The Real Gin Book

A Collection of Classic and Modern Gin Recipes
For Every Occasion

[2nd Edition]

Peter William Parker

Table of contents

Disclaimer

This book is intended to be informative and helpfuland contains theopinions and ideas of the author. The author intends to teach in an entertaining manner. Some recipes may not suit all readers.Use this book and implement the guides and recipes at your own will, taking responsibility and risk where it falls. This work with all its contents, does not guarantee correctness, completion, quality or correctness of the provided information. Misinformation or misprints cannot be completely eliminated.

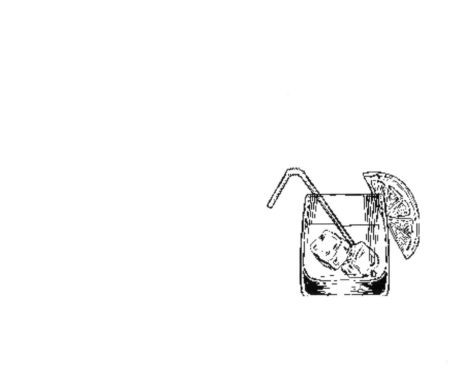

Introduction

Gin. Most people instantly think of the ever-popular Gin and Tonic—and if that's you, then you are in for a big surprise because in reality it is so much more. While Gin may not be your choice of drink if you're looking for something to sip on (and I'm sure Bourbon connoisseurs everywhere will applaud this brave admission!), it is certainly one of the most versatile spirits out there. Its piney and floral flavor profile is thanks to its main ingredient—the Juniper Berry, which makes it an all-around perfect alcoholic addition to a variety of cocktail ingredient combinations.

Whether you are a Gin buff, or simply someone who wants to spice up your cocktail recipe repertoire, there's one thing you need to keep in mind: no two Gins will ever taste the same. The flavor profile of Gins all over the world vary and different brands use different ingredients to make their own unique flavor profile—but the one thing that remains constant is the slightly bitter and piney flavor that comes from the Juniper Berry. This constant, but unique, flavor is what makes Gin a perfect base for so many cocktails—and mixed drinks are definitely the best way to highlight the best parts of your Gin.

One important distinguishing factor to keep in mind is that there are two different types of Gin: Plymouth Gin and Dry Gin. Plymouth Gin delivers a sweeter and smoother taste thanks to the sugar syrup that is added to it while Dry Gin has no additional additives outside of the main ingredients used for its flavor profile—which makes it drier and more bitter. At the end of the day, Gin is a timeless addition to any liquor cabinet, and it is quickly making a comeback as a spirit of choice in the bar scene—and we are sure your taste buds will understand why!

History

The history of Gin can be traced back long before you were even thought of—all the way back to the Medieval Ages (70 A.D. for those of you who would hop on Google to figure out the exact date anyway). Back then the word Gin didn't really exist, so no one automatically thought of the ever-popular Gin and Tonic. Instead, Medieval Italians would steep Juniper berries in wine to make what they coined as a "wine tonic," which they would specifically use for medical purpose.

Later on, during the 16th Century, another medicinal "Gin" (then known as "Genever") emerged among the Dutch. This medicinal mixture was very similar to its Italian predecessor with the only difference being that the Juniper berries were soaked in malt wine in order to mask the piney and bitter flavor that they delivered. By the 17th century, however, the name "Gin" was finally coined, and this is what this Juniper enriched spirit became known as ever since!

Gin is known as a British favorite—in fact, the cofounder of 86 CO. likes to say that the word "Gin" came about because the British weren't able to pronounce "Gen," so that is what it has been known as ever since! In fact, Gin was so popular in Britain that they have an entire period known as the "Gin Craze" thanks to the Corn Laws that were implemented at the time. If you have some free time, you should really look this up--it's really an interesting period in British history that most of us may not even known about, and it eventually led to the Gin Act it England.

To say that Gin is a favorite among the English is an understatement—they literally revolutionized Gin in the 18th century and allowed it to become what it is known as today. After the insanity that ensued after the Gin Craze, Gin makers began using the distillation process that was introduced by Aeneas Coffey. This paved the way to the Gin we know today—clear, delicious, and a perfect base for the cocktail of your choice. London Dry gin quickly became a favorite among the Englishmen everywhere!

Nowadays, Gin is a popular spirit of choice everywhere. It is the perfect base to any cocktail and its pure, piney taste can be appreciated by any spirit lover. While most of us may think of the ever-popular Gin and Tonic when we hear the word Gin, there is so much more to this spirit. From its medicinal origins to the Gin Craze that led to deaths and genuine insanity all over Britain, Gin has an incredibly rich history that encompasses more than the few words we have dedicated to it here.

Production

Gin, as we have discussed quite a bit already, predominately features the Juniper berry. So, for any spirit to be considered a Gin it must feature the Juniper Berry as its focus for its flavor profile and essence. No matter what type of Gin you get, this is the one common gradient that you will find among all of them. Since Gins are known for their unique taste, the alcohol used in its production is not the main event—however, ethyl alcohol must be used as the base when producing a try Gin.

While grain alcohol is used in the production of Gin, it is important to note that Gin differs from Vodka in many ways—this has to be said since so many people often wonder if there is much of a difference between Gin and Vodka. Although Gin uses grain alcohol, that is where the similarities between the two liquors end. Gin can be made from wheat or barley alcohol—and while wheat is the most popular, the Barley bases alternative is a favorite among the Scottish. After all, the Scots are known for their whiskey made of malted barley—so, it makes perfect sense that they would want to feature the barley in their Gin as well!

Once the alcohol base is established, the manufacturers will then add their flavors of choice to the Gin—the most important being the Juniper Berry—through a process referred to as re-distillation or maceration. This is when the flavors will seep into the Gin and give it the unique flavor profile they are trying to achieve. The Gin can be distilled either by steeping the botanicals that are being added (similar to the medicinal origins of Gin) or via vapor infusion.

Steeping the botanicals is a traditional as well as a tried and true method that won't fail. While this process can vary from brand to brand, the basic methods remain the same. Typically, during this process the base is placed in a pot still which contains the alcohol base as well as the main flavor ingredient—the Juniper berries. Other botanicals can be added, depending on the flavor profile the brand is aiming for, and these ingredients will be left to steep for up to 48 hours—it just depends on the manufacturer, and many brands may distill their Gin immediately. When the steeping is done, water is added to reduce the final product into the desired alcoholic percentage required for bottling.

Botanical vapor infusion is a completely different process that is used for brands that want to deliver a gentle but delicious flavor. This process eliminated any need for steeping and the botanicals are actually never even placed in the alcohol base whatsoever! Instead, the botanicals will be arranged within baskets in the pot still. These baskets are located directly above the alcohol base and when it is boiled the botanicals will infuse the base via the vapors that will rise up within the still. Once everything condenses down, water will be added to the final product to dilute it (just like the steeping process) in order to reduce the alcohol strength to that required for bottling.

Types

When it comes to types of Gin, there are 3 different types that need to be distinguished based on European regulations: Gin, Distilled Gin, and London Dry Gin. Those that fall under the "Gin" category are typically neutral in flavor and enriched with additional flavors that are subtle in comparison to that of the Juniper Berry. Those that fall into this category are not flavored during the distillation process, but they are used after—assuming they are even used at all. This is the most cost-effective Gin to produce and the ingredient list is short and simple—but it is also the one with the lowest quality.

Distilled Gin, on the other hand is distilled with the botanicals. It still uses the high proof base alcohol, but the distillation process includes steeping botanicals while it is being distilled—which can be done for up to 48 hours! It is important to note that only specific flavors are allowed to be added, but overall the manufacturer will be able to develop the flavor profile they want to achieve—as long as the Juniper remains the main flavor ingredient.

London Dry Gin is what most people think about when they think of Gin. It has much stricter regulations when compared to the other two and only plant flavors can be used during the distillation process. This type of Gin originated in England—but it is now made all over the world. If you want something with a unique taste., then this is the type of Gin you will want to check out!

While these are the three most recognized Gins out there that doesn't mean they are the only ones! The three we discussed above are definitely the most popular, but there has being quite a few types of Gins introduced since its original inception, and there will most likely be more variations as the years go by as well.

Nowadays, there is also the New Wester Dry Gin (also known as New American Gin), which doesn't feature Juniper as its "main event" and allows other flavors to take over. Old Tom Gin is a sweeter type of Gin that derives its name from street name for Gin back in the 18th Century. This "hipster" Gin has a richer consistency then London Dry gin and is perfect for mixing up your favorite cocktails. Old Tom also has a tint to it and isn't clear like the most popular types of Gins, because it is actually aged in wine barrels—so Old Tom will definitely take you back to what the originators of Gin set it out to be! Plymouth Gin is another one of a kind Gin—and no, it is not just a brand. Plymouth is considered a type of Gin because it has a much higher proof than other Gin—and the fact that it is the oldest distilleries in Europe also carries a lot of weight. If you want a delicious and earthy Gin, then you will definitely love any recipe with Plymouth Gin!

Nosing & Tasting

Nosing and tasting is not as common with Gin as it is with other liquors since it isn't made to be consumed straight. That being said, if you are a true Gin enthusiast you should definitely do both before you use any Gin! Doing so will allow you to notice the subtle differences between the different type of Gins as well as get an idea of the taste they will bring to your cocktails.

While nosing doesn't require you taste any Gin and to do it properly you will simply have to enjoy the aroma of your Gin. For nosing to be done properly you will just have to splash some Gin in your wine glass and breath in the Juniper and botanical aromas that will engulf your senses. While the difference between different Gins may be subtle, if you do this process enough you will eventually be able to tell the different types of Gins apart and distinguish the differences in their ingredients.

When you are done nosing you can proceed to taste your Gin. Not only did you just get to know the flavor profile by enjoying the aroma the Gin lets out, taking a small sip of your Gin will allow you to get the full experience. Since Gin is a high proof liquor that is not made for sipping, it is important to sip slowly and let the little bit of Gin take in mellow in your mouth for a bit before you swallow. This will allow you to not only notice all of the subtle flavors, but also prevent any irritation from occurring if you were to swallow to quickly! If you are new to Nosing and Tasting, don't worry—you will quickly get the hang of it once you do it a few times!

Bar Equipment & Mixing Techniques

Whether you are a novice or expert drink maker, it is important that you be able to perform basic mixing techniques if you want to make any of your favorite cocktails. In order to mix your ingredients properly you will not only need to know how to do it, but you will also need to make sure you have the everything that you need. The most popular and most important mixing tool you will need is the shaker/ Most shakers will come with a strainer—which will keep certain ingredients separate if that is called for in the recipe. If your shaker doesn't come with a strainer, don't worry because you can easily purchase one separately.

Shaking your cocktail is super easy to do once you get the hang of it. Once you have all of your ingredients in you may have to through in some ices, seal it, and shake everything up. Using a shaker will ensure all of your ingredients are properly mixed up—so you can make the perfect cocktail every single time!

While shakers are important, not all of them require that you shake them—which is where the bar spoon comes in. The bar spoon has a really long handle and is perfect for cocktails that require you dilute one ingredient at a time. Lastly, another important bar tool is the shot measuring cup. These are typically double sided, with one side measuring the typical 2 ounce shot and the other measuring a double shot. Some of you may need a traditional measuring cup as well, but most shakers come with measured labels on them, so you probably won't need that at all!

Classic Recipes

Tom Collins

Time: 6 minutes | Amount: 1 cocktail

Ingredients:

- ♦ 60 cl London Dry Gin
- ♦ 10 oz Lemon Juice (fresh)
- ♦ ½ oz Simple Syrup
- ♦ Club Soda
- ♦ Ice
- ♦ 1 Lemon

Preparation:

1. Pour the Gin, lemon juice, and simple syrup into your Glass
2. Fill the cup with the ice.
3. Slice the lemon in half and cut one slice off of it. Divide the rest of the lemon into wedges.
4. Cut a slit into the lemon slice and place it on the rim of your glass.

Gimlet

Time: 5 minutes | Amount: 1 cocktail

Ingredients:

- 7.5 cl Gin
- ½ oz of Lime Juice
- ½ oz of simple syrup
- Ice
- 1 Lime wheel

Preparation:

1. After adding the ice to your glass, pour the Gin, lime juice, and simple syrup into the shaker and shake it well.

2. Pour the cocktail into a glass that has been chilled.

3. Garnish the cocktail with a lemon wheel.

4. *Alternatively, 1 oz of Rose's Sweetened Lime Juice can be used in place of the fresh lime juice and simple syrup.*

French 75

Time: 7 minutes | Amount: 1 cocktail

Ingredients:

- 3 cl Gin
- 9 cl Champagne
- ½ oz Simple Syrup
- ½ oz Fresh Lemon Juice
- Ice
- Lemon Twist

Preparation:

1. Fill the shaker with ice and add the Gin, simple syrup, and lemon juice. Shake it well.

2. Strain the cocktail into a Champaign flute and top it with the Champagne.

3. Garnish the cocktail with a lemon twist.

Gin Tonic

Time: 6 minutes | Amount: 1 cocktail

Ingredients:

- 4 cl gin
- Ice
- 8.5 oz tonic water
- 1 lime

Preparation:

1. Fill a glass with ice and pour the Gin and tonic water into the glass and stir well.

2. Slice the lime in half and cut one slice off. Divide the rest of the lime into wedges.

3. Cut a slit into the lime slice and place it on the rim of the glass. Add in some lime juice by squeezing the lime juice from the lime wedge into the glass.

Negroni

Time: 5 minutes | Amount: 1 cocktail

Ingredients:

- 3 cl Gin
- 3 cl Campari
- 3 cl Sweet Vermouth
- Ice
- Orange

Preparation:

1. Fill your mixing glass with ice and pour the Gin, Campari, and Vermouth. Stir well with a bar spoon.

2. Strain the cocktail into a glass and garnish the cocktail with an orange peel or orange slice.

Dry Martini

Time: 5 minutes | Amount: 1 cocktail

Ingredients:

- 7.5 cl Gin
- 1.5 cl Dry Vermouth
- Ice
- 0.72 grams of Orange Bitters
- Lemon

Preparation:

1. Fill a mixing glass with ice and pour the Gin, Dry Vermouth and orange bitters. Stir well, until the cocktail is nice and cold.
2. Strain the cocktail into a chilled glass.
3. Garnish the cocktail with a lemon twist.

Vesper

Time: 5 minutes | Amount: 1 cocktail

Ingredients:

- 9 cl Gin
- 3 cl Vodka
- ½ oz of Lillet Blanc Apéritif
- Ice
- Lemon

Preparation:

1. Fill a mixing glass with ice and pour the Gin, Vodka, and Lillet Blanc Apéritif and stir it well.
2. Strain the cocktail into a chilled glass.
3. Squeeze lemon juice into the cocktail and rub the glass's rim with it. Drop the lemon in as a garnish.

Simple Recipes

Gin Rickey

Time: 8 minutes | Amount: 1 cocktail

Ingredients:

♦ 4.5 cl Gin

♦ Lime

♦ Club Soda

♦ Ice

Preparation:

1. Squeeze an ounce of lime juice.

2. Fill glass with ice and pour Gin and lime juice. Top it off with club soda.

Gin Buck

Time: 5 minutes | Amount: 1 cocktail

Ingredients:

- 4.5 cl Gin
- Lemon
- Ginger Ale
- Ice

Preparation:

1. Squeeze an ounce of lemon juice.
2. Fill glass with ice and pour Gin and lime juice. Top it off with Ginger Ale. Lightly stir.

Salty Dog

Time: 5 minutes | Amount: 1 cocktail

Ingredients:

- 4.5 cl Gin
- 9 oz Grapefruit Juice
- 20 grams of coarse sea salt
- Grapefruit
- Ice

Preparation:

1. Wet the rim of the glass and rim it with the coarse sea salt. Fill the glass with salt.

2. Pour the Gin and grapefruit juice into the shaker. Shake well.

3. Pour the cocktail into the glass and garnish it with a slice of grapefruit.

Bee's Knees

Time: 10 minutes | Amount: 1 cocktail

Ingredients:

♦ 6 cl Gin

♦ ¾ oz Lemon Juice

♦ ½ oz Honey syrup

♦ Ice

♦ Lemon Twist

Preparation:

1. Fill the shaker with ice and add the Gin, lemon juice, and honey syrup. Shake it well.

2. Pour the cocktail into a glass that has been chilled.

3. Garnish the cocktail with a lemon twist.

4. *The honey syrup is composed of ½ a cup of honey and ½ a cup of water. Pour these into a small saucepan. Use medium heat and stir it well until it is well blended.*

Hanky Panky

Time: 5 minutes | Amount: 1 cocktail

Ingredients:

- 4.5 cl Gin
- 4.5 cl Sweet Vermouth
- 2.5 grams Fernet-Branca
- Ice
- Orange

Preparation:

1. Fill a mixing glass with ice
2. Pour Gin, Sweet Vermouth, and Fernet Branca into the glass. Stir well with a bar spoon.
3. Garnish the cocktail with an orange twist.

Southside

Time: 7 minutes | Amount: 1 cocktail

Ingredients:

♦ 4 cl Gin

♦ ½ oz Lime Juice

♦ ½ oz Simple Syrup

♦ Club Soda

♦ Ice

♦ Sprig of Mint

Preparation:

1. Place the sprig of mint into the shaker and add the lime juice and simple syrup. Muddle the mint well.

2. Pour the Gin into the shaker and fill it up with ice. Shake well.

3. Fill a glass, with crushed ice. Strain the cocktail into the glass.

4. Stir well, until slush begins to form. Top with club soda.

5. Garnish with mint.

London Light

Time: 5 minutes | Amount: 1 cocktail

Ingredients:

♦ 6 cl Gin

♦ ½ oz Grapefruit Juice

♦ 1 oz Pomegranate Juice

♦ Club soda

♦ Grapefruit.

♦ Ice

Preparation:

1. Fill glass with ice. Pour Gin, grapefruit juice, and pomegranate juice.

2. Top the cocktail with club soda.

3. Garnish the cocktail with a grapefruit twist.

Lemon Berry

Time: 5 minutes | Amount: 1 cocktail

Ingredients:

♦ 7.4 cl Dorothy Parker Gin

♦ 1 oz of Lemon Juice

♦ 0.5 oz Blueberry Grenadine or puree

♦ Seltzer

♦ Ice

♦ Blueberries

♦ Lemon

Preparation:

1. Put ice into a win glass to the brim.

2. Add everything to the shaker, EXCEPTthe seltzer and shake vigorously. Strain into glass.

3. Top up with the seltzer, garnish with the blueberries and lemon.

Lying Lady

Time:5 minutes | Amount: 1 cocktail

Ingredients:

- 6 cl of The Botanist Gin
- 1 oz of Cointreau
- 1 oz of Fresh Lemon Juice
- 1 Egg White
- Grated Orange Zest
- Ice

Preparation:

1. Add the gin, Cointreau, lemon juice, and egg white to a shaker and shake.
2. Add the ice and shake some more.
3. Strain over a chilled coupe glass and grate orange zest on top.

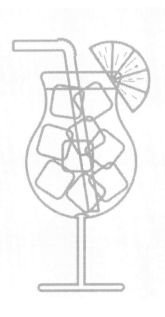

Lavender and Lemon

Time:5 minutes | Amount: 1 cocktail

Ingredients:

♦ 4.4 cl Uncle Val's Botanical Gin

♦ 0.5 oz Lemon Juice

♦ 0.25 oz Lavender Simple Syrup

♦ Lemon Wheel

♦ Lavender Sprig

♦ Ice

Preparation:

1. Add all of the ingredients to an ice filled shaker and shake.

2. Pour into a coupe glass, add a lemon wheel and a sprig of lavender.

Refreshing Recipes

London Lemonade

Time: 5 minutes | Amount: 1 cocktail

Ingredients:

- 6 cl Gin
- 5 oz Lemonade
- Ice
- Lemon

Preparation:

1. Fill a glass with ice. Pour the Gin and lemonade. Stir well.
2. Garnish with a lemon wheel.

Parisian Frizz

Time: 5 minutes | Amount: 1 cocktail

Ingredients:

- 3 cl Bombay Sapphire Gin
- ½ tspn of Cranberry Hibiscus Syrup
- 0.5 oz of fresh lemon juice
- 3 oz of brut champagne
- Ice

Preparation:

1. Add the gin, cranberry hibiscus syrup, lemon juice and ice to a shaker and shake.

2. Strain the cocktail into a chilled champagne glass and top up with brut champagne.

3. Cranberry Hibiscus Syrup:

    - 500ml of Water

    - 500ml of white sugar

    - 3 cups of hibiscus flowers

    - 2 cups of sliced fresh cranberries

    - Heat everything together for 12 minutes, stirring well.

    - Take the pan off the heat and strain through a sieve to remove all the solid bits. Leave in the fridge until chilled.

Speedwell Cooler

Time: 10 minutes | Amount: 1 cocktail

Ingredients:

- 4.5 cl Gin
- ½ oz Aperol
- ¾ oz Simple Syrup
- ¾ oz Lemon juice
- 1 oz Watermelon Juice
- ¼ tsp Absinthe
- Ice
- Salt
- Cucumber

Preparation:

1. Pour the Gin, Aperol, simple syrup, lemon juice, watermelon juice, Absinth, and a dash of salt into the shaker. Shake well.

2. Strain the cocktail into a glass.

3. Peel the cucumber and garnish the cocktail with a cucumber peel.

Floradora

Time: 10 minutes | Amount: 1 cocktail

Ingredients:

- 6 cl Gin
- ½ oz Ginger Syrup
- ½ oz Raspberry Syrup
- ½ oz cl Lime Juice
- Club Soda
- Ice
- Raspberries

Preparation:

1. Pour the Gin, ginger syrup, raspberry syrup, and lime juice into the shaker. Fill with ice and shake well.

2. Fill a glass with ice and strain the cocktail into it.

3. Top the cocktail with club soda.

4. Garnish it with a raspberry.

5. *Alternatively, you can make your own raspberry syrup.*

Rhubarb and Strawberry Collins

Time: 7 minutes | Amount: 1 cocktail

Ingredients:

- 4.5 cl Gin
- ¾ oz Rhubarb Syrup
- ½ oz Aperol
- ¾ oz Lemon Juice
- ½ oz Strawberry Juice
- Club soda
- Ice
- Lemon wheel

Preparation:

1. Pour the Gin, ginger syrup, Aperol, lemon juice, and the strawberry juice into the shaker. Fill with ice and shake well.

2. Fill a glass with ice and strain the cocktail into it.

3. Top the cocktail with club soda.

4. Garnish it with a lemon wheel.

Ramos Gin Fizz

Time: 7 minutes | Amount: 1 cocktail

Ingredients:

- 6 cl Gin
- ½ oz Heavy Cream
- ½ oz Lime juice
- 1 oz Lemon Juice
- 1 oz Simple Syrup
- 2.5 grams orange flower water
- 1 egg white
- Club Soda
- Ice
- Lemon wheel

Preparation:

1. Pour the Gin, heavy cream, Aperol, lime juice, lemon juice, simple syrup, orange flower water, and the egg into the shaker. Shake well without ice.

2. Fill the shaker with ice and shake well.

3. Strain the cocktail into a glass and top it off with club soda.

4. Pour some club soda into the shaker to get any remaining egg white and pour it into he glass.

Silver Cloud

Time: 7 minutes | Amount: 1 cocktail

Ingredients:

- 3 cl Gin
- ½ oz Peach Shrub
- ¾ oz Lavender Syrup
- ½ oz cl Lemon Juice
- 1 egg white
- Ice
- Lavender Sprig

Preparation:

1. Pour the Gin, peach shrub, lavender syrup, lemon juice, and egg white into shaker. Shake well.

2. Add ice and shake well again.

3. Strain the cocktail into a glass and garnish with the lavender sprig.

4. *The peach shrub will require 12 oz of chopped, pitted peaches, 6 oz of sugar, and 6 px of apple cider vinegar. Combine the peaches and the sugar in a bowl and muddle them. Add the vinegar and let it set for a day or 2 before straining.*

Kyuuri Hana

Time: 5 minutes | Amount: 1 cocktail

Ingredients:

- 6 cl Gin
- 3 cl Cucumber Vodka
- 2.2 cl Sour Mix
- ½ oz Simple Syrup
- Lemon
- 6 mint leaves
- Cucumber
- Ice

Preparation:

1. Pour the Gin, cucumber Vodka, sour mix, and simple syrup into the shaker. Fill with ice and shake well.

2. Fill a glass with ice and strain the cocktail into it.

3. Garnish it with 2 to 3 cucumber slices.

Fall Fizz

Time: 5 minutes | Amount: 1 cocktail

Ingredients:

- 6 cl Gin
- ¼ oz lemon juice
- Agave nectar
- Sparkling Apple Cider
- Thyme
- Apple slice

Preparation:

1. Pour the Gin, lemon juice, agave nectar into a cocktail shaker and shake well.

2. Pour it into a high ball glass, top up with the sparkling apple cider.

3. Garnish with the thyme and apple slice.

Apricot Passion

Time:8 minutes | Amount: 1 cocktail

Ingredients:

- 3 cl Gin
- 2 tsp Sieved Apricot Jam or Glaze
- 3 cl Passion Fruit Juice
- 1 cl Lime juice
- Crushed Ice

Preparation:

1. Add crushed ice to a glass and the jam/glaze on top of the ice.

2. Pour the gin over the apricot jam/ glaze and mix with a swizzle stick or spoon, until the jam/glaze is dissolved.

3. Add the passion fruit and lime juices, more crushed ice and serve.

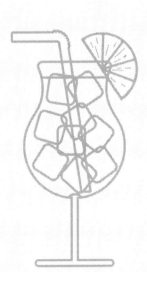

Gin and Mint

Time: 7 minutes | Amount: 1 cocktail

Ingredients:

- ♦ 5 cl Gin
- ♦ 2 washed sprigs of mint
- ♦ 1cm thick slice of cucumber, cut into quarters
- ♦ 10 cl elderflower cordial
- ♦ Small mint sprig
- ♦ Lemon slice
- ♦ Ice

Preparation:

1. Add the gin, elderflower cordial, the washed mint sprigs and cucumber to a glass jug or shaker.

2. Stir, while squashing the mint and cucumber enough to release their juices.

3. Strain into a tall glass filled with ice and garnish with the small mint sprig and lemon slice.

Exotic Recipes

Rosie Lee

Time: 8 minutes | Amount: 1 cocktail

Ingredients:

- 4.5 cl Gin
- ½ oz Rose Petal Syrup
- 1 oz Lychee Juice
- ½ oz Freshly Squeezed Lemon Juice
- 1.5 grams Angostura Bitters
- Ice
- Lemon

Preparation:

1. Fill the shaker with ice and pour the Gin, rose petal syrup, Lychee juice, lemon juice, and the Angostura bitters over it. Shake well.

2. Strain the cocktail into a teacup that has been filled with ice.

3. Garnish the cocktail with a wedge of lemon.

4. *To make the rose petal syrup, infuse 8 oz of simple syrup with a handful of rose petals for a total of 48 hours. Strain it before using it in your cocktail.*

Bramble

Time: 5 minutes | Amount: 1 cocktail

Ingredients:

- 6 cl Gin
- 1 oz Lemon Juice
- ½ oz Crème de Mure
- 2 tsp of Simple Syrup
- Ice
- Lemon
- Blackberries

Preparation:

1. Fill the shaker with ice and pour the Gin, lemon juice, and simple syrup in. Shake well.
2. Fill a glass with ice and strain the cocktail into it.
3. Top with the Crème de Mure and garnish with a blackberry and lemon wheel.

Gin Daisy

Time: 7 minutes | Amount: 1 cocktail

Ingredients:

- 4.5 cl Gin
- 1 oz Lemon juice
- Prosecco
- 5 grams Grenadine
- ½ tsp Sugar
- Ice
- 1 Maraschino Cherry
- Orange slice

Preparation:

1. Fill the shaker halfway with ice. Pour the Gin, lemon juice, grenadine, and sugar into the shaker. Shake well.

2. Strain into a glass or champagne flute and top with Prosecco.

3. Garnish the cocktail with the Maraschino cherry and orange slice.

Elderflower Gin Fizz

Time: 5 minutes | Amount: 1 cocktail

Ingredients:

- 8 cl Elderflower Gin
- 6 cl St. Germain
- 2 oz Apple Juice
- Soda Water
- 1 oz Lime Juice
- Ice
- Cucumber

Preparation:

1. Fill the shaker with ice. Pour the Gin, St, Germain, apple juice, and lime juice in. Shake well.

2. Fill a glass with ice and strain the cocktail into it. Top with soda water.

3. Garnish with cucumber spears.

Dotty Ginger

Time: 5 minutes | Amount: 1 cocktail

Ingredients:

- ♦ 1 oz Dorothy Parker Gin
- ♦ 1 oz Dolin Blanc
- ♦ ½ oz Giffard Lychee
- ♦ ½ oz ginger
- ♦ ½ oz lemon
- ♦ 1 makrut lime leaf

Preparation:

1. Pour all ingredients into a cocktail coupe glass and garnish with the makrut lime leaf.

Gin Sunset

Time: 8 minutes | Amount: 1 cocktail

Ingredients:

- 3 cl Gin
- 3 cl Orange Liqueur
- ½ oz blackcurrant fruit juice syrup
- 2 oz chilled peach nectar
- Crushed Ice

Preparation:

1. Fill a mixing glass with ice and pour Gin, orange liqueur, and peach nectar. Stir well with a bar spoon.

2. Fill a martini glass with the crushed ice and strain the cocktail into the glass.

3. Drizzle the syrup over the top and serve.

Corpse Reviver No. 2

Time: 6 minutes | Amount: 1 cocktail

Ingredients:

♦ 2.2 cl Gin

♦ 2.2 cl Cointreau

♦ 2.2 cl Lillet Blanc

♦ ½ oz Lemon Juice

♦ Absinthe to rinse

Preparation:

1. Fill the shaker with ice and pour the Gin, Cointreau, Lillet Blanc, and lemon juice in. Shake well.

2. Rinse a Martini glass with the Absinthe. Strain the cocktail into the glass.

White Lady

Time: 5 minutes | Amount: 1 cocktail

Ingredients:

- 6 cl Gin
- 1.5 cl Combier or Cointreau
- ½ oz Lemon Juice
- 1 Egg White

Preparation:

1. Fill the shaker with ice and pour the Gin, Combier or Cointreau , lemon juice. And egg white into the shaker. Shake well.

2. Strain the cocktail into a Martini glass.

Ginny Weeds

Time: 15 minutes | Amount: 1 cocktail

Ingredients:

- ♦ 6 cl Gin
- ♦ 1oz of Yellow Chartreuse
- ♦ ½ oz of Lemon Juice
- ♦ ½ oz of Lime Juice
- ♦ 0.75 oz of tarragon tea syrup
- ♦ Tarragon leaves
- ♦ Ice

Preparation:

1. Add all the ingredients together in a shaker, add ice and stir.

2. Strain the cocktail into a Martini glass.

3. Garnish with the tarragon leaves.

4. Tarragon tea syrup:

   - 2 cups of water

   - ½ cup of sugar

   - ½ cup of fresh tarragon

   - Combine all in a medium saucepan and bring to a boil. Allow to cool before using.

4 Way Smash

Time:8 minutes | Amount: 1 cocktail

Ingredients:

- 2 cl gin
- 2 cl brandy
- 2 cl rum
- 4 cl orange juice, freshly squeezed
- 2 cl lemon juice
- 1.5 cl almond syrup
- 0.5 cl sherry
- Ice

Preparation:

1. Add the gin, brandy, rum, orange juice, lemon juice and almond syrup to the shaker and shake.

2. Pour the cocktail into a tall glass of ice and top up with the sherry.

3. Be careful with this quadruple hit!

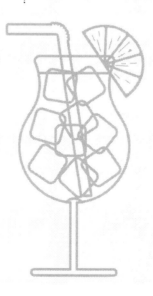

Fizzy New Orleans

Time:5 minutes | Amount: 1 cocktail

Ingredients:

- 4.4 cl Gin
- ½ oz Lime Juice
- ½ oz Lemon Juice
- 1¼ oz Simple Syrup
- 2 oz cream
- 1 small egg white
- 2 dashes of fleurs d'orange
- 1oz club soda
- Ice

Preparation:

1. In an ice filled shaker, everything except the soda and shake.

2. Remove the ice and shake vigourously to ensure the egg white and cream have properly combined. Should be silky and smooth.

3. Strain the cocktail into a high ball glass and top up with soda.

Modern Recipes

Shifting Sands

Time: 5 minutes | Amount: 1 cocktail

Ingredients:

- 4.5 cl Gin
- 1.5 oz Grapefruit Juice
- 2 tsp Maraschino Liqueur
- ½ oz Lemon Juice
- Club Soda
- Ice
- Grapefruit

Preparation:

1. Fill the shaker with ice and pour the Gin, grapefruit juice, Maraschino Liqueur, and lemon juice on top. Shake well.

2. Fill a glass with ice and strain the cocktail into the glass. Top with club soda.

3. Cut the grapefruit into wedges and garnish the cocktail with a wedge.

Modern English

Time: 7 minutes | Amount: 1 cocktail

Ingredients:

- 7.5 cl Gin
- ½ oz Maple syrup
- 1 Lemon
- Ice
- 1 Pear
- Cinnamon Stick

Preparation:

1. Cut the lemon into wedges and cut the pear in half.

2. Pour the maple syrup into the shaker and squeeze the lemon wedges into the shaker. Slice up the pear and put it in the shaker. Muddle these ingredients together.

3. Fill the shaker with ice and add the Gin. Shake well.

4. Double strain the cocktail into a Martini glass and garnish it with the cinnamon stick.

Valentino

Time: 5 minutes | Amount: 1 cocktail

Ingredients:

- ♦ 6 cl Gin
- ♦ 1.5 cl Campari
- ♦ 1.5 cl Sweet Vermouth
- ♦ Ice
- ♦ Orange

Preparation:

1. Fill the shaker with ice and pour the Gin, Campari, and Sweet Vermouth into the shaker. Shake well.

2. Once it has been shaken, stir the cocktail with a bar spoon.

3. Strain the cocktail into a Martini glass and garnish it with an orange twist.

Saturn

Time: 5 minutes | Amount: 1 cocktail

Ingredients:

- 4 cl Gin
- ½ oz Passion Fruit Syrup
- ½ oz Lemon Juice
- 0.75 cl Falernum
- 0.75 cl Orgeat
- Ice
- Edible flower of your choice.
- Parasol (mini umbrella)
- 1 orange

Preparation:

1. Fill a blender with crushed ice and add the Gin, passion fruit syrup, lemon juice, falernum, and orgeat. Blend the ingredients well until the cocktail is smooth throughout.

2. Pour the cocktail into a glass and garnish it with the parasol (mini umbrella), edible flower, and orange peel. Serve with a straw.

3. *If you want to make your own passion fruit syrup you can do so by mixing 18 cl of simple syrup and 3 cl of passion fruit puree.*

Midnight Prayer

Time: 6 minutes | Amount: 1 cocktail

Ingredients:

- 4.5 cl Gin
- ¾ oz St. Germain Liqueur
- 1 tsp Crème de Violette
- ¼ tsp Orange Bitters
- Lemon
- Ice

Preparation:

1. Pour the Gin, St. Germain liqueur, Crème de Violette, and orange bitters into a mixing glass. Fill the glass with ice and stir the cocktail well with a bar spoon.

2. Strain the cocktail into chilled cocktail glass and garnish it with a lemon peel.

Garrick Club Punch

Time: 45 minutes | Amount: 1 cocktail

Ingredients:

- 7.5 cl Gin
- 12 cl Maraschino Liqueur
- 2.5 oz Seltzer Water
- 8 oz Lemon Juice
- 4 oz Fine Sugar
- 4 Lemons
- Ice

Preparation:

1. Peel the 4 lemons with a fruit and vegetable peeler, make sure to avoid the lemon's white pith.

2. Put the lemon peels in a punch bowl and add the fine sugar. Muddle the peels and let it sit for half an hour.

3. After the 30 minutes are up, pour the lemon juice into the punch bowl. Stir the sugar and muddled ingredients until the sugar dissolves completely.

4. Pour the Gin and the Maraschino liqueur into the bowl and stir well.

5. Fill bunch bowl with ice, about halfway, and pour the club soda. Stir well.

6. Serve in punch glasses or highball glasses. Garnish with a lemon wheel.

Elderflower Collins

Time:5 minutes | Amount: 1 cocktail

Ingredients:

♦ 5 cl of gin

♦ 0.70 oz lemon

♦ 0.3 oz sugar syrup

♦ 0.3 oz elderflower cordial

♦ Club Soda

♦ Ice

Preparation:

1. Add all ingredients to a cocktail shaker and shake.

2. Pour into an ice-filled glass, top up with soda and add a sprig of your favorite herb as a garnish.

3. To up the ante, swap out the club soda for some sparkling wine to make an Elderflower Royale.

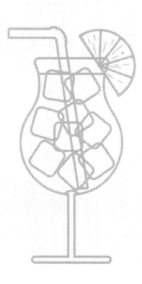

The Foamy One

Time:5 minutes | Amount: 1 cocktail

Ingredients:

- ♦ 5 cl sloe gin
- ♦ 2 cl lemon
- ♦ 1.5 cl sugar syrup
- ♦ 2 cl egg whites
- ♦ Ice
- ♦ Rosemary sprig

Preparation:

1. Shake everything together, including the sprig of rosemary.

2. Remove the ice and shake again for maximum foam.

3. Pour into a pretty wine glass and serve.

Monkey Gland

Time:5 minutes | Amount: 1 cocktail

Ingredients:

♦ 6 cl Gin

♦ 1 oz Orange Juice

♦ ¼ oz Grenadine

♦ Dash of Absinthe

♦ Orange Slice

♦ Ice

Preparation:

1. In a chilled cocktail glass, swirl the absinthe around to coat the glass. Dump any excess absinthe.

2. Take ice and fill a cocktail shaker, add the gin, orange juice and the grenadine and shake well.

3. Strain the cocktail into the absinthe'd glass and garnish with orange slice.

Extravagant Recipes

The Final Say

Time:5 minutes | Amount: 1 cocktail

Ingredients:

- ♦ 2.2 cl of Martin Miller's Gin
- ♦ 0.75 oz of Green Chartreuse
- ♦ 0.75 oz of Luxardo Maraschino Liqueur
- ♦ 0.75 oz Lime Juice
- ♦ Ice

Preparation:

1. Add all ingredients to a shaker and shake.
2. Strain the into a coupe glass.

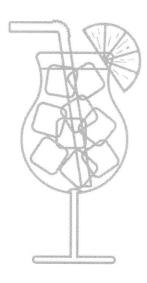

Blue Milk of Tatooine

Time: **7 minutes** | Amount: **1 cocktail**

Ingredients:

- 6 cl Gin
- 1 oz Coconut Cream
- ¾ oz Pineapple Juice
- ¾ oz Lime Juice
- 1.5 cl Blue Curacao
- ½ oz Orgeat Syrup
- ½ oz Vanilla Syrup

Preparation:

1. Fill the shaker with ice and pour the Gin, coconut cream, pineapple juice, lime juice, Blue Curacao, Orgeat syrup, and the vanilla syrup into the shaker. Shake well.

2. Strain the cocktail into a glass, or the glass of your choosing.

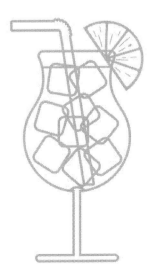

Kumquat Smash

Time: 7 minutes | Amount: 1 cocktail

Ingredients:

- ♦ 6 cl Gin
- ♦ 1 oz Lemon Juice
- ♦ 1 cl Maraschino Liqueur
- ♦ 3 Kumquats
- ♦ Nutmeg
- ♦ Ice

Preparation:

1. Place the Kumquat in the shaker and muddle them.

2. Pour the Gin, lemon juice, Maraschino liqueur, and nutmeg into the shaker. Add ice and shake well.

3. Fill an Old Fashioned glass with ice and double strain the cocktail into it.

4. Garnish with the other 2 kumquats.

The International

Time: 7 minutes | Amount: 1 cocktail

Ingredients:

♦ 3 cl of Junipero Gin

♦ 3 cl of King's Ginger Liqueur

♦ 0.5 oz of Round Pond Meyer Lemon Syrup

♦ 0.75 oz Fresh Lemon Juice

♦ Splash of Soda Water

♦ Luxardo Maraschino Cherry

♦ Ice

Preparation:

1. Add all of the ingredients, except the soda, to a shaker and shake.

2. Pour over ice and top up with the soda and the maraschino cherry for garnish.

The Pale Rider

Time: 8 minutes | Amount: 1 cocktail

Ingredients:

♦ 4.5 cl Gin

♦ 1.5 cl Blanc Vermouth

♦ 1.5 Fino Sherry

♦ 1.5 grams Angostura Bitters

♦ 1.5 grams Orange Bitters

♦ 5 grams Farigoule Thyme Liqueur

♦ Ice

♦ Lemon

♦ Absinthe

Preparation:

1. Pour the Gin, Vermouth, Fino Sherry, Angostura Bitters, Orange Bitters, and the Farigoule Thyme Liqueur into a mixing glass. Fill it with ice and stir the cocktail well for 30 seconds with a bar spoon.

2. Rinse a glass with the Absinth and strain the cocktail into the glass.

3. Garnish the cocktail with a lemon peel and serve.

Tazza di Vita

Time: 7 minutes | Amount: 1 cocktail

Ingredients:

- 3 cl Gin
- 6 cl Amaro
- 2.5 oz Simple Syrup
- 2.5 o Lime Juice
- Club Soda
- 2 Mint Sprigs
- Cucumber
- Ice

Preparation:

1. Peel and chop the cucumber and set aside 57 grams for the cocktail.

2. Add the simple syrup 1 sprig of mint, and 57 grams of cucumber into the shaker. Muddle the ingredients.

3. Pour the Gin, Amaro, and lime juice into the shaker and fill it with ice. Shake well.

4. Fill a tall glass with ice and strain the cocktail into it.

5. Top the cocktail with soda water and garnish the cocktail with a cucumber wheel and mint sprig.

Cosmopolitan 1934

Time: 7 minutes | Amount: 1 cocktail

Ingredients:

- ♦ 4.5 cl Gin
- ♦ 1.5 cl Cointreau
- ♦ 1 oz Lemon Juice
- ♦ 1 oz Raspberry Syrup
- ♦ Dehydrated Orange Wheel
- ♦ Ice

Preparation:

1. Fill a mixing glass with ice and pour the Gin, Cointreau, lemon juice, and raspberry syrup. Mix well with a bar spoon.

2. Strain the cocktail into a large coup and garnish it with orange zest and a dehydrated orange wheel. Alternatively, you can use a fresh orange peel if you don't have a dehydrated one on hand.

3. *If you want to make your own, homemade, raspberry syrup you can d to the following: Add 4 cups of water, 4 cups of sugar, and 1 cup of water to a saucepan. Bring the ingredients to a boil, with the heat setting on low. Simmer the sauce for five minutes. Strain it once it has cooled down and you will have plenty for future use!*

Smuggler's Cove Straits Sling

Time: 8 minutes | Amount: 1 cocktail

Ingredients:

- 4.5 cl Gin
- 7.5 cl Bénédictine
- ¾ oz Lemon Juice
- ½ oz Cherry Heering
- ½ oz Demerara Syrup
- 1.5 grams Angostura Bitters
- 1.5 grams Orange Bitters
- Lemon
- Club Soda
- Ice

Preparation:

1. Pour the Gin, Bénédictine, Lemon Juice, Cherry Heering, Demerara Syrup, Angostura bitters, and the orange bitters into a mixing glass. Fill it with ice and stir the ingredients well with a bar spoon.

2. Fill a glass with ice and strain the cocktail into the glass. Top the cocktail with club soda.

3. Slice the lemon up and garnish the cocktail with a lemon slice.

4. *The Demerara syrup can be made by adding 3 cl of Demerara sugar and 1 oz if water into a saucepan. Turn the heat to low and stir well.*

Sergeant Pepper

Time: 6 minutes | Amount: 1 cocktail

Ingredients:

- 7.5 cl Gin
- 1 tsp Raw Sugar
- 1 Lime
- 1 McIntosh Apple
- 12 Black Currants
- 8 Black Peppercorns
- 1.5 grams Orange Bitters
- Ice

Preparation:

1. Cut the apple in half. Peel and cube one half of the apple and slice the other.

2. Put the cubed apples in the shaker and muddle them.

3. Put the lime, sugar, Black Currants, orange bitters, and black peppercorns in the shaker. Muddle all of these ingredients together.

4. Pour the Gin in the shaker and fill it up with ice. Shake well.

5. Fill a glass with ice and double strain the cocktail into the glass.

6. Garnish the cocktail with an apple slice.

Violet Concord

Time:15 minutes | Amount: 1 cocktail

Ingredients:

`
- ◆ 1.5 cl of Violet infused Gin
- ◆ 2.21 cl of Amaro (Amaro Braulio)
- ◆ 1 Oz of Homemade Concord grape juice
- ◆ .5 Oz of Pink grapefruit juice
- ◆ .5 Oz egg whites
- ◆ Ice

Preparation:

1. Violet infused gin: Take one bottle of dry gin, add one tablespoon of violet tea and infuse for 10 mins.

2. Mix all the ingredients in a shaker, and dry shake for 30secs .Add some ice and shake again for a further 10 secs.

3. Pour into either a martini or a "Nick and Nora" glass, with a double strainer.

Cockatoo Cocktail

Time:7 minutes | Amount: 1 cocktail

Ingredients:

- 4.4 cl Ford's Gin
- 0.75 oz Giffard's Pamplemousse
- 0.25 Oz Green Chartreuse
- .5 Oz Lime Juice
- 2 drops Tiki Bitters
- Ice

Preparation:

1. Add all of the ingredients to a shaker and shake.

2. Strain into a cocktail coupe glass.

3. Garnish with peels of lime and grape-fruit.

Holiday Recipes

Holiday Dinner

Time: 8 minutes | Amount: 1 cocktail

Ingredients:

- 6 cl Thyme and Saffron Infused Gin
- 1/3 cup Turkey broth Syrup
- 1.5 cl Apéritif
- 1.5 grams Orange Saffron Bitters
- Celery Bitters
- Ice
- Thyme
- Crouton
- Saffron Sprig

Preparation:

1. Fill a mixing glass with ice and pour the Gin, Apéritif, turkey broth syrup, and the orange saffron bitters to the glass. Stir the ingredients well with a bar spoon.

2. Add celery bitters to a glass and swirl it around well to coat the entire glass.

3. Strain the cocktail into the glass and garnish it with Thyme sprig, Saffron sprig, and a crouton.

4. To infuse the Gin, add 10 sprigs of Thyme and 20 sprigs of saffron to a bottle of gin. Let it set for a day (24 hours) and strain the it to get all of the solids and the sprigs out of the infused Gin.

5. *To make the turkey broth syrup pour 2 cups of turkey broth into a saucepan. Add pepper, salt, garlic powder, 2 sprigs of saffron, and 3 sprigs thyme to the saucepan. Heat it on low and bring all of the ingredients to a simmer for 10 minutes. Strain it and add 16 oz of sugar and some more pepper. Whisk the ingredients until all of the ingredients dissolve—this should hold up for about a week.*

Under the Mistletoe

Time: 5 minutes | Amount: 1 cocktail

Ingredients:

- 6 cl Gin
- 1 oz Simple Syrup
- 2 oz Cranberry Juice
- 1 oz Club Soda
- Orange
- Thyme
- Ice
- Cranberries

Preparation:

1. Slice the orange into half wheels.

2. Place two half wheels and 7 cranberries into a glass. Muddle the ingredients.

3. Pour the Gin and Simple Syrup into the glass. Fill it with ice and stir the ingredients well with a bar spoon.

4. Top the cocktail with cranberry juice and club soda.

5. Stir the cocktail with a Thyme sprig and leave it in the glass as a garnish. Pop in 3 additional cranberries into the glass as a garnish.

Hey Bulldog!

Time: 5 minutes | Amount: 1 cocktail

Ingredients:

- 6 cl Gin
- 3 cl Chambord
- 1.5 cl Peppermint Schnapps
- 7 up or Sprite
- Ice

Preparation:

1. Pour the Gin, Chambord, and Peppermint Schnapps into a glass. Fill it with ice and stir well.

2. Top the cocktail with 7 up or sprite.

Hot Gin Punch

Time: 15 minutes | Amount: 1 Punch Bowl

Ingredients:

- 3 Cups of Gin
- 3 Cups of Madeira Wine
- 3 oz Honey
- 1 oz Lemon juice
- 3 Cloves
- 1 tsp Brown Sugar
- 1 tsp Cinnamon
- Nutmeg
- Pineapple
- Lemon
- Orange

Preparation:

1. Grab a large saucepan and pour the Gin, Madeira Wine, honey, lemon juice, cloves, brown sugar, a pinch of nutmeg, and 3 chunks of pineapple into the saucepan.

2. Turn the heat on low and simmer the ingredients in the saucepan for 20 minutes.

3. Slice the orange up and pour the hot punch into a punch bowl. Garnish the punch bowl with the orange slices and 3 cloves.

4. Serve the punch in teacups or mugs.

Winter Cranberry Gin Fizz

Time: 7 minutes | Amount: 1 cocktail

Ingredients:

- 6 cl Gin
- ½ oz Cranberry-Rosemary infused Simple Syrup
- Ginger Ale OR Ginger Beer
- 2 tsp lime juice
- Ice
- Rosemary
- Cranberries

Preparation:

1. Place ¼ of a cup of the cranberries in the shaker along with the juice. Muddle the two ingredients together.

2. Pour the Gin, simple syrup, and fill the shaker with ice. Shake well.

3. Strain the cocktail into a glass and top it with the ginger ale or the ginger beer.

4. Garnish the cocktail with a sprig of rosemary and some cranberries.

5. *To make the Cranberry-Rosemary infused simple syrup add 4 oz of any unrefined sugar, 4 oz of water, 2 sprigs of rosemary, and 4 o of fresh or frozen cranberries into a small pot. Turn the heat on high and stir the ingredients. When it starts to boil, lower the heat to medium and stir until the cranberries begin to pop and the sugar starts to dissolve. Once that happens, turn the heat off and stir the ingredients some more. Let the syrup cool and stick it in the refrigerator or freezer until you need it.*

Spiced Holiday Gin Punch

Time: 12 minutes | Amount: 1 Punch Bowl

Ingredients:

- 30 cl Gin
- 30 cl Pimms No. 1
- 4 cups Ginger Ale
- 1 cup of chilled Chai Tea
- 1.5 cups Orange Juice
- 2 tbsp Lemon Juice
- Anise
- Clove
- Frozen Cranberries
- Lemon
- Oranges
- Rosemary Sprigs
- Ice

Preparation:

1. Pour the Gin, Pimms, ginger ale, Chai tea, orange juice, and lemon juice into the punch bowl. Mix all of these ingredients well.

2. Cut the lemon and orange into slices. Spike all the lemon and orange slices with cloves.

3. Add ice to the punch bowl. Add the spiked lemon slices, spiked orange slices, cranberries, and anise.

4. Garnish the punch with rosemary sprigs.

5. Serve in glasses.

Merry Xmas Cocktail

Time: 5 minutes | Amount: 1 cocktail

Ingredients:

- 3 cl Gin
- 1 oz Cranberry Juice
- 1tsp Lemon Juice
- Club Soda
- Ice
- Cranberries

Preparation:

1. Fill a glass with ice and add the Gin, cranberry juice and lemon juice. Stir well with a bar spoon.

2. Top the cocktail with soda water and garnish it with a few dried or fresh cranberries.

Saucy Christmas

Time: 5 minutes | Amount: 1 cocktail

Ingredients:

- ♦ 6 cl Gin
- ♦ ½ oz Fresh Lime Juice
- ♦ 2 tbsp Cranberry Sauce (with NO whole berries)
- ♦ 2 dashes of Peychaud's Bitters
- ♦ Sprig of Rosemary
- ♦ Ice

Preparation:

1. Add gin, lime juice, bitters, ice and the cranberry sauce to a shaker.

2. Shake well for a minimum of 30 – 45 seconds.

3. Using a mesh strainer, pour into a chilled coupe glass.

4. Release the rosemary sprig aromas by smacking it between your palms, and place on top of the cocktail.

The New Year

Time: 5 minutes | Amount: 1 cocktail

Ingredients:

♦ 6 cl Gin

♦ ½ oz simple syrup

♦ ½ oz Lemon Juice

♦ Champagne

♦ 1 sprig rosemary

Preparation:

1. Add the gin, simple syrup and the lemon juice to the shaker.

2. Shake and then double strain into a large coupe glass.

3. Top up with champange.

4. Garnish with sprig of rosemary.

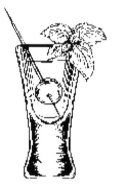

Legal Notice